Everything Broken Up Dances

# Everything

# Broken

# Up

# Dances

James Byrne

Tupelo Press

North Adams, Massachusetts

Library of Congress Cataloging-in-Publication Data

Byrne, James, 1977–
[Poems. Selections]
*Everything broken up dances* / James Byrne. -- First paperback edition.
    pages ; cm
ISBN 978-1-936797-66-0 (softcover : acid-free paper)
I. Title.
PR6102.Y745A6 2015
821'.92--dc23

                              2015016240

Cover and text designed by Bill Kuch. Text composed in ITC Giovanni,
Insignia, and PikesPeakZero. Cover art: "Wall," photograph by Jeffrey Levine.
Used with permission of the artist.

First paperback edition: December 2015.

Tupelo Press
P.O. Box 1767, North Adams, Massachusetts 01247
Telephone: (413) 664–9611 / editor@tupelopress.org / www.tupelopress.org

Tupelo Press is an award-winning independent literary press that publishes fine
fiction, nonfiction, and poetry in books that are a joy to hold as well as read.
Tupelo Press is a registered 501(c)(3) nonprofit organization, and we rely on public
support to carry out our mission of publishing extraordinary work that may be
outside the realm of the large commercial publishers. Financial donations are
welcome and are tax deductible.

Supported in part by an award from
the National Endowment for the Arts

*for Sandeep Parmar*

# contents

## Foreword

What is the language of poetry that responds to twenty-first century wars? What modern-day Goya will paint the horrors of bombardment in Syria, Libya? What modern-day Brecht will insist that in dark times too, there must be singing?

To say that James Byrne is one of the best UK poets of his generation is to underestimate him. For in these poems conscience gathers scraps of voices in destroyed cities, always in search of "the other," in moments after blackout, in that darkness where the eye begins to see.

Sometimes I think Byrne is writing our times' wailing songs, like those poets of the past who once came to wash and bury the bodies of the dead. He has that kind of *claritas*. He searches for truth without illusions, with full awareness that "still the fool's face stares from the smashed mirror."

He isn't the sort of a poet who goes to war-torn countries for the romancing of disaster. His aim is to balm ("bell of your name, Ali"), to see and honor in each of us the "lifeboat of ribcage."

It is his empathy that I love, the healing in poems such as "Trinkets," the embrace of the fractured, the wrinkled, in poems such as "Old Men of Skopje Old Town."

And yet, just as I think I understand this poet's perspective, he always surprises me. I want to call him a brilliant civic poet, but the page turns and Byrne stuns me with his take on family ("blind on entering the masked ball / that is marriage"), on sobriety of private existence ("Dreams are / embroidered by people that exist"). Whatever his subjects are, it is his voice that haunts me, as he dares us to imagine the world "as if / Adam died before he had / time enough to recast man's / beastliness among animals." A poet who attains such clarities is rare.

Ilya Kaminsky

# 1977

*Star Wars* premiered as they cut the exiguous flap of my umbilical.

THE KING IS DEAD ran *The Herald* and the midwife handed over the genesis
of my unfledged, unwhimpering body.

In the carrycot of my mother's arms, hissing privately with birth,
I cried nothing, confessed nothing.

It was the year of the snake and *The Spy Who Loved Me*—
the year Zulfiqar Bhutto was ousted by the Bond villain ul-Haq.
The year Steve Biko was clubbed to death in custody.

Fidgety among the hangings, my grandfather peered down longingly
    for 90 minutes
at the pitch below the hospital where Rangers were leading Wanderers.
A Rangerette herself, when I was born my mother asked the Doctor
    for the score—
'It's a classic match: eight fingers, two thumbs.'

75,000 fans lined the streets of Memphis for the King's funeral.
500 million tuned into their small screens
as the Queen's Jubilee carriage trundled up The Mall.

My father was late to the maternity ward.
He arrived bearing a thin deck of lilies, whitely inflamed from their sprigs.

It was the year President Carter pardoned draft dodgers and George Willig
(a.k.a. 'The Human Fly') climbed the World Trade Center.

I was speechless and ready to alight, preserved by a flambeau of luck.

This was the year Sadat became the first Arab leader to visit Israel seeking
    a peace deal—
the year my brother, on hearing the altarpiece of our house break in its glass,
shelved us together, under the bed.

'When will it ever stop?' I heard one voice whisper to another.
My mother scooped up my egesting mess from the floor.

The year ended in a clappering of bells.

Amnesty won the Peace Prize.
The Cold War was inscrutable.
On and on it went.

Everything Broken Up Dances

## Postcards

All night the Commander,
With a high, baronial laugh,
Peels a scent of sweet mandarin
From the waist of a waitress.
They will heap mud over her eyes.

The boy soldiers entered the house
And rounded up the market gardener,
His two sons, his fiery old grandfather,
And shot them where they crouched
In their shadows.

A mother counts penitence on her rosary.
The baby in her stomach grows eyes.

At the tribunal, the army secretariat
Blamed Mother Nature herself—
A great and sudden simoom that caused
The sorry fire. And nobody can condemn
The amnesiac history of the wind,
Or the amnesiac history of fire.
They did not mention the bolted doors,
Or the gasoline tanks strewn like tooth stumps.
The frost-bound face of a government judge
Deemed the newly widowed witnesses
Over-emotional. Unreliable.

The village has been stripped to a wound.
Two scorpions scrap in a crucible of sand—
The question mark of their tails singeing the air.

The boys have made a giant playhouse
From the rubbled stanchions of the razed compound.
Two kid Generals line up teams
For a game of Guns vs. Swords.
And then the swashbuckle
And then the rat-tat-tat from their mouths
To make the guns seem real
For the onlooking fathers of the Revolution
Who pick sides, shout and cheer.

At the far wall of the bombed-out mosque,
A prayer tannoys back the Prophet's take
On forgiveness during times of anger.
But the muezzin dragged in the dust by his collar
Now cracks and cracks again
Against the tantara of his voice.

These are two of the postcards that could not be sent.
Beetle-nib eyes under the slivery sheet of a moon
That quakes over her sea-wrinkled face.
The profile of the skeleton
Who visits her by night,
His mechanical arms
Upraised, still
Pleading
Mercy.

At the military mountain base,
Five men are led down its steep side
Then deep into the shallows of a grove.
Nobody will tell the story here.
The mountain is quiet and infinite.
The buzzards silent in their appetites,
Only the olive leaves hiss back to the sky.

## One / Another

One sighs heavily down the telephone
Another pours the assassin's quicksand

One leaves the garrison lonely as a bullet
Another fills white tubs with kerosene

One is surveyed from the border glass
Another guards against the darkness of trees

One clinks to the enemy's thimble
Another fantasizes death in a flyway

One slugs the sitter at his pianoforte
Another takes shade under a fig tree

One discerns bloodiness from the siren
Another brandishes the manacles

One juggles dust between his hands
Another combusts the basecamp

## Wild Desert Thyme

*for Sandeep*


For your sprigs of wild desert thyme
we convoy to the sea-gardened city of Sabratha
ghostwalking Greco-Roman walls
kitchen-quarters
dungeons
the trembling concave of its amphitheatre
gold as dusk
re-casting the invisible chorus
and backdropping away
to the distant Maghreb
the cooled winter gulf
where I dip my feet
amid the rockscrub

then afterwards
led through the white museum
where my face sang
in the glasshouse of the tragic actor
and was neither healed nor lured
by the attending lyre of Bacchus
or Concordia's matted scarf of serpents
I sat in the mosaic hall of the three graces
smelling out the tarry bitterness of human meat

※

A daydream woken off by gunfire
(another deferred wedding?)
hurried to the bus
in a cloudrack of dust
to relative calm
the stricken village of Surman
brown limbs of shelled apartments
still wearing the massacre effect
our creaturely sicknesses
old as Jupiter's beard tresses

exact middle of the sun-burnished street
a hunched woman harries sacks of grain
our driver honks her to a fright
and she spills half the carryweight
then turns to level back at us
staring from under a black shawl
open and enormous in her silence

For your wild desert thyme
we take the checkpoint road
beneath the Nafusa mountain
(an old Romanic route
straight as tightened rope)
on one side burst a hundred-yard of camels
triumphantly riderless
and from the smeary west window
all the way to the checkpoint
a scrapyard of tanks
ditched in the roadside's gullet
their armaments plundered
overturned khaki
bleeding bulletholes
and scorched 4x4s piled
five high

potent as ash in the dustpath
in the chancelleries
of war and hunger

⁂

The checkpoint soldiers
of the Free Libya Army
draw Kalashnikovs
nervous in a kind of antique fear
circling the vehicle at first
until we pay them off
with victory signs
and Ashur's laugh of the honeybee

on the lassoing road of the mountain
WELCOME TO YEFREN
graffiti'd in English
Berber and Arabic
THANK GOD FOR EVERYONE'S SAFETY . . .
PUT UP YOUR HEAD . . . YOU ARE FREE LIBYA . . .
trucks on stilts
cracked gas-pipes
and grey-sprayed wheelbarrows
outside the hardware shop
where the shopkeeper taps his pen
on the window grill
and a boy fills a barrow with dead mortar shells

⁂

For your wild desert thyme
the Algazeer re-hoist their flag
(rainbow of yellow blue red and green)
the Algazeer who have farmed this mountain
for eight hundred years
and who survived the war

by living in ancient caves
beneath the stonebase of their ancient city
Gaddafi banned the Algazeer
burnt their flag
cut the food and water
says Sālim
spiderishly nimble on the tumbled rocks
pointing to a road
that does not meet and has not met
for eight hundred years

and it is from this road
that I kneel down
past the abandoned bootlegger path
where the olive trees sing
from the desert's hymnbook
and the caves hold the scent
of a just-skinned carcass
and the synagogue rises
from a camouflage of sand

The taste of the future
is history
tethered inside a green box
a volcano of perfume
wind-sculpted
embalmed with leaves
like a tree . . .
open it?

## Mallajah

Mute for minutes—keeffak—ana bikhayr—note guttural Rs—gobbets
on Hikmet—genius or personality—the butterfly insignias of
Darwish—not a *Burden*—non-verbal—bricabrac Arabic—can be a
blessing—scan the table for unpayable translators—sh'kran habibi—
cannot learn a language just by hearing it—Spanish maybe—sh'kran—
wide glossy smile—all I can say—sh'kran habibi—drinking mate
through a scolding straw—gets rid of Arak—gets in teeth—tamam—
medicine *and* breakfast—need water—you stir it like this—clockwise
is anticlockwise—like the alphabet—sh'kran—what better life than
the life in *this* valley—whiff of Mediterranean over the olive grove—
where are you from, Hamad—hypnotism in gasblue eyes—what he
said makes perfect sense but cannot be translated into English—
time suspended by a conjurer's trick—literally then—the children of
my first painting never forget to smile—my teeth are cleaner here—
my teeth rot every day in Lebanon—skin like the valley's rockface—
remember where you stand—the men of three villages built this
festival—stone by stone—Rasha's father fell carrying these rocks—
could be the seventh century—over one thousand will fill this valley
tomorrow night—half or more from three villages—there—there—
there—we've moved on but the point is still to be made—nothing rots
on its own, says Hamad—poor translation—do you like Tartous—can
attract waiters but not yet order any food—what about Damascus—
walked up Qasioun in strawburning heat—didn't Cain slay Abel up
there—holiest of balconies—Telemnin on one side—the Old City
islanded in the distance—gold and whitelight—pleated gold—
can't tell you that now can I—what about the barbed-wire road
with the green tower roadblocked by soldiers—off the map—don't
wait to eat—*eat*—bread is the life of the table—sh'kran—I offer the
basket to a gaptoothed boy—calls me Sahibi—face of one pure note—
wears half the paint lost from the canvas—twill of reds pinks oranges
greys—titled: *An Olive Tree Lit by Thorns*—sh'kran—tamam—preface /
footnote / trio—everything said in a museum of accents—haven't read

Mafouz—haven't listened to Fairuz driving through the dark valley at night—outsider—outmajoritied—but we are all family here—all same—octopi of embraces—cigarette—sh'kran—Amira hides spirit tears—divorce pending—man has to give consent—three years—*three years*—you would do fine if you didn't have a girlfriend—red apple cheeks—Firas circles the room with a mothy dance—the far end of the table is singing—clefts of banned Syrian folk—Sammi's mother transforms into a veritable Venus—how to pronouce that—*Yaall daar*—spits like a soothsayer over her tahini bowl— her name means longest night of the year—you see how it is—sh'kran—President Assad like a king with a million eyes, a million ears—translation: please habibi—not the poem about Iraq

## Variations on Darkness

*How slowly dark comes down on what we do.*
Theodore Roethke, *from* "In Evening Air"

1.

If you drink from the shuck of the storm
you will always be tainted by its darkness.

2.

The lacquered surface of the canal at night
is darker than the darkest shroud of Jesus.

3.

One thing darker than the rose's shadow
—the cold fire of the roses after thunder.

4.

Far murkier than possession—the shiphold
shackled to the hells of human darkness.

5.

When the rusted machete cut back the cane
it sharpened darkly in the emperor's silence.

6.

Amnesially waiting in the cinema's darkness
—it cannot be separated out from loneliness.


7.

The panmongolist was so afraid of the dark
he asked to be buried in a candlelit coffin.


8.

A death-pecked cry darkens the entire city
and is hoisted through the shrieking world.

# Shaqti

Shaqti opens the gold reckoning case of his mouth to knock back coffee.

'My teeth are only worth a concubine's room,' he says.

Dented blue-grey eyes laughing over Ray-Bans. London '77, Zurich '79.

A Tripolitanian café in the hills of Bohemia, '88–90.

Shaqti the shot bird, the tour guide who cannot recover his way.

Who, without water, would not drink from the sea,

And without food, would not catch a fish.

Shaqti who swallowed a mouthful of blood on the death of King Idris.

Who mourns that every country cannot move as one spirit:

'I am alone and my country is alone in all the tribes of its country.'

Shaqti still drinking coffee as if it were a carafe of metaphysical wine,

Still seventeen waving a blooded flag from a blazing oilrig.

Who chides the Sudanese as conscripted hirelings.

'These scavengers won't go home,' he says,

Breaking the allegro of a tour through the Old City,

'Now Sudan doesn't want them and Africa doesn't want them.'

Two schoolchildren pin a wriggling Sudanese boy to the wall

And they hold him there and spit out their demands.

Shaqti at the water hyacinth with the tears of Apollo.

Shaqti the unpaid engineer who appears humble and kind

But has bargained too much and lost too much.

Who strokes the face of a MISSING poster at Hammamkbir and says:

'Look at this boy. He is my son.'

# Epitaphs for a New Century

1.

on the count of GO run for your life.

apply elevated heels for a better view

and remember no one tips the gallows.

in television county ancient stones

weigh us down. the axe cools beside

new recipes for double-butter muffins.

rise from the armchair to hear agony

creak. nothing exists beyond the bridge

of your nose. minutes refined by sand.

anchoresses in limousines. old trades.

flesh money. from spiders under glass

to backbone tumors—shared breath—

enough for a pulse in the rough houses.

behind thick red smoke the informants

appear proud as parents at a home plate—

each wears a silver watch on his left hand.

2.

mirrorlicker. you snooze you win.

a loud selfie to cure worrywarts.

the dust particulates. no tallying

the bodycount. scene in Damascene.

hearse ears. silence is a threshold—

the buzzfeed echoes like hills.

who wouldn't want to be counted out.

two slats fell from the roof last night—

almighty crashes. inner-hymns.

what else is there to write about.

flowers in vases. chain-link fences.

how summer grasses drink the rain.

so much for shovelling up shadow.

on Which Poet Are You I got Walcott.

corvine skeletons in frosted tents.

package secrecy of the mail queue.

3.

take a tree but it won't water the apple.

build cities from mud, and culture with

money. death counts beyond numbers.

outside The Spastics Society a white goat

chained and puerile tries to lick its own

arsehole. air was the cleanest weapon

of all. woof goes the one-eyed century.

nailed to wounds and in barrack-shadow

the kid chewing chole sells old postcards.

ideodeities for the tourist's hands that

dance as if attacked by hornets—to ask,

how much will it cost to get you out

of my face? the unholy cow is butchered

the markets emblemize life and there's

no friendlier way to sacrifice chickens.

pay up or put up and know your place.

4.

milk drains off and friendships creak

with the past like an old bullock cart.

the dream of the cobbler possesses me.

Duchamp in Acheron or Dostoyevsky

in London—we want to live in the sea

that is not our home. no patron saints

only laser-eyed community directors.

the kids are turning into chrysalides.

work—*wrekan*—meant to persecute.

its variant *wreaked*. robots of *rabota*,

love not sleep lest you come to poverty.

the man our village calls Polish Mick

trembles curtains and twitches the whip.

it's action that makes a community.

the good shoe will fit like a readymade.

what cannot be sold to us is fog-logic.

5.

aquariums dance well not the fish.

winter early this year and so much

bad weather as if it were between us.

why is it some painters suffer more

when painting breezes while others

can hear seeds clicking in a field.

Van Gogh's sunned orchard beside

tile cats laving in late afternoons.

Shostakovich suckerpunched by the 14th

same as for Nietzsche patting stirrups.

activist or terrorist but do not blemish

the human canvas. be still and spectral

as woodsmoke or grubby as old jokes.

like the one where Guy Fawkes laughs

at his own funeral—the most honest man

who would ever set foot in parliament.

6.

girl among the hawthorns wait for me.

the bluebells are speaking in Spanish.

let's clear the table for a game of cards.

forgetfulness devours. thunder is luck.

there's always more kindling to burn—

stave off the heat by closing shutters.

practice the disclosure of photographs.

in the bright fields we have shat upon,

in the boiled-down effigies of nature,

open-air aviaries. blood on hessian.

what does it mean to return to a native

place. pennants of memory. a river.

family trees still logjam the Goree

caste fishermen steady up spears.

so much for the redemption of Libra

rising. the hidden filigrees of gold.

## To a Dispossessing Friend

Have ready the hivestone of a preliminary cell,
the battle orders and the four truths of Buddha.

Have ready the Doctor's radiophonic fever note—
I must receive it loud like an instructional rocket.

Have inventories of day duty on a ropepull—
I will adhere to the two-bucket humanity solution.

Have in mind the winning patience of the fox.
Decry the peacock headdress, the dog muzzle.

I will arrive like a memory buried in deep seed.
I want to drink from the fisheries of pure water.

I promise to reveal the simple self more in public.
I must oar away the nihilist's cheap accoutrements.

Have ready the accelerant portrait of my father.
I will be the criminal who got caught and walked.

## The Opponent

Though it is a scarlet day my opponent wears his topcoat in the park. Old squirmy enthusiast, always nodding out of sight from the pack; today he is an onlooker in redwood shade. With a cool apprehending finger he points up to the springy torso of a beech tree. I study its green hydra-headedness, and there, among the forked branches, an American Redstart, nested, and so it appears, unable to fly from its black and orange overalls. *Share our impediments,* asks the opponent in his broad, larval accent and wide, footsore smile. *Tell me,* I retort, *which of you lives greater today: autocrat or lizard.* A long Arian cackle before he readopts the face of an Aquarian. Does evil cluster inside evil. Was he born with a wick for trapdoors. I sneaker to a foothold, cup the Redstart, and with a quick movement of my wrist snap down on its neck. For a moment, so brief, too brief, something bordering desire remains inside the bird until the final flick-flack release of its fantail. *Beautiful* says the opponent, with a calm, iniquitous stare. *Almost exactly as if I would have done it.*

## No Smoking

Pulling away residually from old devotions,
I keep my brow low and watch the domino
bones capsize: encoded snow on black slate.
Falling, the equation misses my forebrain—
its inventorying of the foamy bar menu,
divided / sub-divided by the burly ruckus,
where a man smokes from his supernatural
mouth and another coupons the jukebox
with charred screams. The falcon landlord
flashes at my hard-bitten nails, a combustible
look. He's a gimcrack, menacing the anecdotes,
sure that mine will brink me out and over—
outsider to the unspillable smile of the maître d'
who asks 'what will it be?' and cannot tell me.

## Saint Patricks

*for Patrick T. Byrne*


1.


hawkeye over Midtown
      the clannish banner squadron
pauses at KILKENNY
      its homespun flourish
          immaculately routined
the timewarped flagmaster
      a ringer for McGuinness
          re-pressed in IRA slack-suit
he pushes his neo-Celt
        drummerboy son
          forward
        to XFactor the solo
    Boys of the Old Brigade
pride in the hand
      like a scorpion's tail
from barricaded wings
      spectatorial drum of applause
         stallion nerve in the salute
      *oh father why are you so sad*
two generations of Kilkennys
        venerated
        raised by force
attending skyscrapers
      a cave for the bodhran

2.

the latest Bloomberg blooper
       via leprechaun facepaint
              tricolor sarong of young Erins
                    sexed like a unicorn
              pale jade in rare sun
       they have lugged the Magners casket
                 of a green icebox
       for merry-merry shapeshift
       mock-Hibernia
Fifth Avenue pre-profit
              cruciforms cut through
                    the nebbish crowd
              cranny round the bandstand
Father Harris
       Guinness-robed
green-laureled
       thumps the baldpated mic
buffet for Christendom

3.

family I don't know
      historical manholes
            graves ajar from open ledges
a voice calling for a son
        à la Cavalcanti
              embalmed under Dis
no Virgil to decode the thresh of inquiry
      more hearsay on a saintless Patrick
      a namesaken father
     scorned to infectious velum
            in the family atomic
who disowned his father in turn
        until the larvae of cremation
how he adjusts an English-blue collar cuff
     for the anguish of interviews
the middenly socio-conundrum
     NO BLACKS NO DOGS . . .
later sniffing at pints of London Pride
     the too colorful Union Jack
        the awkwardness of reunions
I pendulum to his uncle-sluggishness
       wondering what germinates
          under the plank-stiff boy
      in the passport photograph
Paddies bi-cameral in Lexington green fields
       under cenotaph stacks
         where the sun's retinue
    swivels back
     Dis-enflamed
too brightly
    I whinny through
      the cure to escape East

4.

past Celtish windowpanes
            for a nostalgia pass
                    Muldoon's Pub
                    McDevitt's Bar
I hedge on the freshened thorn
                            (Blakean Celt)
                whose cameo address
            I stopper in for heights
                    four-leafed / eight-leafed
to relieve myself
            from the back bar
                    ravelling in a toilet scene
heavy looks
                    past / future
                    present
                    in the bloodstream
now geographic
                    toe-stubbing on sham-rock
                            out-shamaned
                    a simpleton sideglance
                    to cast my green nets
                    at the whirlpool
there
I discover
myself
by minutes
                    waterpocketed
                    clovered
                    the toxic green wine of the East River

## Windows (Alfresco)

1.

Your pilot-eye
               (contract signatory)
     effronts a hand
        waving broadly
   from the closed window

     like a shipmast
        tannyoying its landflag

     trumpet of enthusiasm
     to watch my step through

            the checkmate street
            in the checkmate city

2.

Derivations:

> clay screens of Melinda
> > (our adjoining neighbor)
> traverse leaden shadows—

the blown glass shelf
> > through the firestairs
> half-annulled by grilled iron

outside the bronze temple
> of the grey casement window
> > her windcatcher tremors

elvish little life in there
> spindle of endeavor

> > > moving about the room
> > > in knitting-needle quietness
> > > > sun-streaked

> > > —as if turned by zodiac
> > > weather appendages—

her lamentable wraith gown
> > her grandeur of speechlessness
> > > her stillness from the neck

the tightness
> of her cheeks
> > prune-like
> in the brown wine
> > of a low dusk

she folds
over folds
    a drift of white linen

        bowing and disappearing

        flushed clean by the light
           to a lamp of water

3.

Corporate jaw
        cubed /
        percentaged
in the burial chamber
        of a flatscreen window

trammelled axle points secure
        liquid chaos
—uncultivating mystiques—

        in the gilled fishbowl boardroom
        (where the fish are hooked /
            tenterhooked)

steam tunnels under the jalousie
        an austerity broker
        card-cutting silhouettes—

the tall-suited man
his back turned
        to a fixed        double-hung
        mock-palladian
        window

        the mise-en-scène—

        a licked finger
            pointing
        to the blacked-out
        white man

        an accusatory digit
            barrelled in shadow

        a holotype
        salute-firm    fired
        like a gun

4.

music room window of the upper brownstones
where practice makes                    practice

　　　　a perennial child
　　　　malingers at the bay ventricle

　　　　　　　　curates
　　　　　　frame-by-frame
　　　　　　　　an off-key viola

—instrumentals eluding the planned course—

　　　　clumsy stringwork
　　　　　　afflicts the beehived
　　　　　　　　punitive maestro

　　　　she who would raise the split
　　　　　　　　cane of a tuning fork
　　　　　　wipes her sleeve
　　　　　　　　in the light

　　　　unwilling protégée
　　　　—her paisley-eyed apertures—
　　　　　　unfussed

recomposing herself
　　　　for Brahms bodycheck

sitting in the open cinema
　　　　　　of her paralysis

　　　　　　　　*again*　　*again*
*again*

## *from* The Caprices

*after Goya*

*They say yes and give their hand to the first comer*

For whom the story does not end well
is not liberated. Swooned to man,
blind on entering the masked ball
that is marriage. Dark suitors among
the packrat crowd. One foot points
towards an illegitimate altar, the other
heeled, but offering no resistance.
Complicit is she who would not demur.

*Here comes the bogeyman*

To summon a father from the shit
of roots and odors. *Abuso funesto.*
Call him by names that do not exist,
he follows you like a sun's shadow.
The annex of his echo is sanguinary
and a pricked finger tastes of his blood.
Fathers and sons become men of rivalry,
boys do not know beyond their good.

*Nanny's boy*

Snug-ugly, raised on nanny's hams,
made of eyes so as not to see sense.
Grown insufferable, child as man,
carousing in drag on stag weekends.
If family is the world's first true woe
it is followed by the family corrupted.
Play piggywiggy with him, let him go
to the market to find himself, she said.


*Two of a kind*

Enkindled: one loves as the other,
is as vile as the other. The coxcomb's
limp grin turns the Duchess of Alba,
five years shy of her widowy frown.
Synchronized clocks of their faces,
hands timed to the geomagnetic field.
Who can legislate for attractiveness?
Who knows as another person feels?

*Nobody knows himself*

Wear a face to look more like yourself.
Clothes, flesh, and voice are all false.
I am the mystery occasioned as myself,
compound volatile, a cat chewing mouse.
Self-absconded, avidly elsewhere,
I sleep silent as ink. Ancestral breath
blows clean the candle. Dreams are
embroidered by people that exist.


*Even thus he cannot make her out*

He is a tree lost in his own wood.
She is a tree chiseled by a knife.
He has no body, only a giant head
and glowers from a monocled eye.
Now stooped at her shoulder, as if
from constipation, rake and crooner,
inimically flirtatious. Sing of this,
gentlemen, the song you cannot hear.

*They carried her off*

Anjashna, who are the they is he
and is you: possessors enact their law.
Woman as cargo glass. *La muger qe
no se sabe guardar.* Man is impure
as the dirt he would taint you with.
Before the schoolgirls in Chibok
were carried off to Sambisa forest
all those wearing trousers were shot.


*Tantalus*

Wake me up when it is all over.
Like Dean Martin in the demo studio,
only your voice is ever really there.
Dispassionate in sotto voce, Tantalo,
rumoring with grubbers at the market,
yet so cold as to make stew of his son.
Eternally thirsting, ghosting Hades,
crush my love under a tombstone.

*Love and death*

World falls to pieces between men.
Darkness spars inside a lighthouse.
We master nothing, divisibly human,
urgently sweating, a handful of earth.
Laughter condensates frosted glass,
wet flames gasp for love and death.
Until the final drawing of swords,
you are at the threshold of a life.

## The Humming Lady

The humming lady arrives
in a smiling orange smock
and orders from the waiter
a plate of overripe oranges,
peeling off the snowwebs
into a red-blanketed napkin.
She hums a centuries-old
Romany tune, which I half-
recognize as the fugue to
my own death (and so it
must be her own death).
Through orange mist and
beneath a brown-greying
fringe, she appears to half-
recognize both of our lives
and turns (out of politeness?)
towards an invisible volta.
Clear pearl of eye where
I thank smilingly, pleased
at the new tempo, its cheer
turbinal about the room,
unsealed maternally from
the willow of her throat.

## Isabella Stewart Gardner in Venice

A Zorn,

      (though his irregular patroness directs the scene)

EXT:    *Blue sashays under the Palazzo balcony.*
INT:    *The blizzard of a citrus gown strung with pearls.*

      . . . Backlit by the fire-floating Grand Canal,
      a Jamesian Dove clawing at shutter glass,
      lapsed Second of the balletomane in her fanned arms,
      flush-faced, as if from aftersex with some Venetian gadabout.

At her feet, a curtsey of red flowers . . .
      loose oil of a thrown carnation?

          'Come out—all of you—
          this is too beautiful to miss . . .'

The eye looks on and through and looks away.

# Improvisations for Adam-Baiting

*Rock*

whinnying snakeskin
to the lachrymal girl
fronting the moshpit
who exempts herself
in stretching to touch
the scarred geography
of secondary birth—
water to the sleeping
lifeboat of a ribcage
encases her orphanhood
and the rhino-horned
six-stringed encore is
ejaculatory whenever
he plays the final solo


*Heart*

bar where dead men
go to die and the dandy
barman stiffs Chuck
another carafe of wine
under the thorn-tether
of his brow and droopy
eyes—for Chuck who
dies piecemeal when
pre-electing men over
women—revelling in
himself made mystical
announcing to the bar
'when I knew women
I knew my own heart'

*Fire*

clinkered to fire how is it
women live to the strike
of a matchbox while men
grow more crooked—as if
Adam died before he had
time enough to recast man's
beastliness among animals—
fire from a dowry's length
lit by the original mother-
fucker who is matricidal
as the sun burns—like
Coriolanus saving Rome for
one woman—Volumnia—
her hushed cry of fire

*Sex*

Eve's newest contortion
refolds her like a paper
dragon (man's nature is
indulgent as breath itself)
gentlemen do not read
gentlemen's magazines
yet the broadsheets are
colonially impervious—
Purves's western frippery
as if sex were the fulcrum
of Asia—not the cockroot
of my neighbor planted
towards the TV screen
across a hallway of glass

*Naked*

or as if from skin's tunic
to a lovejoy's messabout
or a walking targetboard
sinisterly affranchised in
gold Armani and who in
ipod silence doesn't hear
how *she had it coming* or
how the Styx holds open
to the bling of heaven—
love cools under the net
that swelters her—as if
she might fashion deeper
than a handful of cloth or
something to be reaped


*Bread*

in the sweat of your face
you shall eat bread means
a fair day's work earns
a fair-floured loaf not
being told to *calm down
dear* because it's only
a (testosterone) commercial
where the Cabinet is full
of dormboys playing men
born to rule—who would
dock dry an entire country
or a single mother's right
to be free from the turd-
baking of errant husbands

*Money*

Belle de Jour calls it self-
empowerment at three-
hundred pounds an hour
but the shot-silk Burmese
teens treading bath foam
in Patpong might suggest
otherwise (if allowed to
speak at all) curious maybe
at the banking of after-
dinner-speaker rates and
the callgirl's uncontrollable
smile—tithed as they are
to trafficking and the plow
of weekend millionaires

## Cloud

A musketry of small children
inoculated with play now point
beyond the scabrous row of trees
to a palpitating hypocritical sky

Their source a cloudbowl's trifid
pinnated / needled / rooked with rain
lacquering the brightly dazed avenue—
foray of cloud with its mottle-grease
rasping over the baldly uncaped

Fearless children with pink tongues
poked out peaceably as if they were
harmonized by the frigate cloud
who wheezes slowly south to sea

# Burden

*for Yusef Komunyakaa*

Downtown, already snagged between two countries, I make stock
footage for a London return—block after block, hobbling in unwalkable
shoes, uptown from the Ground Zero memorial where, today, Obama
laid wreaths and tousled the head of Cannizzaro: a one-year-old boy
on 9/11. 'You look just like your father,' said the President, 'sorry he's
gone.' Death stalks the day like a dog, whistles from news-racks, *Time*
marks Osama with a red-drip cross on his head: 'Special Report: The
End of Bin Laden.' Later, in Lillian's House, at the reading on West
10th, I peel back strips of plaster: no comfort these Xtra Comfort
leathers. In 'Warhorses' a soldier suicides on a grenade and is blown
to the limbs. 'He just dove on the damn thing, Sir.' Of the surviving
battalion one tries to jigsaw the confetti of the dead man's stomach,
another stuffs pieces of him into a rag bag. Death stalks the day like
a dog. In my cheap shoes I shuffle for a pipe on Patchin Place with
the student they nickname 'The Green Godmother.' Her brother will
be reposted from Korea back to Texas next week. Like him, exilic,
multiplex, she feels bound to Korea—the returning nerve to retrack
a mother who gave her up for adoption. 'I don't know where to live
anymore,' she says, but her 'Sea Legs' thesis is already signed away, to
which we cheer and are gone—the light querying us from Brando's
old room. Blurred into Sixth Avenue, a hornet row of taxis, my face
pained in the tourist bus window. 'For those who can walk away,
what is their burden?'

# Conscript

*for Hasko Hasko*


A mandatory sentence
the artist at the face of his enemy

MECHANIZATION

who perfects    (for futility)
rerun after rerun—

>how to rise out of the featureless sand
>cranking a gunsight for the corps guard


At the iron-dry Qasioun
>in khaki fractal-camps
the mind's rookery      its mineral vision
>double-camouflaged


Here
>halting and saluting to the slinkhole
>of a General's opalescent eyeball

>for the well-groomed glock chamber
>the chemical flourish of bootshine

your blackish and bovine five-legged Kurdistani hogs
>still sharply recline under blue statues of blue women

the red centerline of your house
>braying with laughter

unavailed by the stasis

## Fragments for Ali

lend me a syllable
      from Assyrian ash
            from the ashes of Ishtar

unruffle my birdsnest ignorance

           Ali

you who brothered me there
like a son and bronzed silver
      into figures of amity

in the desert path above Tartous

      through salt tides
      and toothsucking sand

the bell of your name

           Ali


        ※


hardbreathing of pebblestones
                  promises
        lost to the iron-shore sea

the upturned hulls
      of fishing boats
                 wet with life
        as if hope struck
             suddenly
and was bundled out by the sun

*※*

winter ices the weathervane
ditch-lilies
          in the Alawite district
where your ailing mother lives—
                    reproach of the tank's eye
          death-chills
                    tingling the museum gates

and somewhere beyond the pocked wall
and somewhere beyond the spyglass
among shelled-out newbuilds
and frail city stanchions

          your son walks
                    the herded miles

*※*

blood in the jasmine
sweat of death
                    . . . . . . . . . . . . . . . . . . . . .
                    . . . . . . . . . . . . . . . . . .
how do new buds grow
from beheaded flowers?

*※*

families hide out for months
                    in their homes
insomnia-riven

betrayed by the dark
　　　　and the painted
irreality of television

relatives names
　　　　on blacklists
in windows　　　　purloined
　　of the old familiar faces


※


where in these Mallajah hills
is the lamb of your niece?

　　sorrow of the olive grove
　　bones that conspire in the Queiq river


※


　　an amphitheatre
　　　　labored over
　　brick-by-brick
　　　　now cordoned

　　where the villagers
　　　　cannot be sure
　　of the informers
　　　　from the mob

　　school-less children
　　　　stare out from
　　pillars of rock
　　　　to the distant

grey Mediterranean—
mesh of Europe

✳

to speak is a game of chess

terror in the telephone
where no one appears to
listen

dread of breath
silence that roars

## Bones and Blood

Where might the sitting council sit
on Martyrs Road? Will they bud
more lime-green shoots to spout
over the military garden? No calm
in the hedgerow along the dark mile
of the street, the bolt of a gunbarrel
juts from the grills like a baited snake.
The guards remain vigilantly poised,
wide-eyed in a weft of hammocks.
Why—for over thirty years—a 32°
chill still pervades the pagoda road?
And why—after years of mopping up
bones and blood—do the stray dogs
still cower, lapping at betel juice?

## Are you in the hills, Ashur?

Are you in the hills, Ashur?
the prophecies you wrote
read predatorily acute
there at the blade shaft
amid battle-shrapnel
connecting peace war
to holy war to bureau war
these eternal strictures
handiwork for bribe cuts
to mass in the censoring
scythe over Green Square
still-shot for Libyan TV
agenda-set cutaways
strip cold an entire family
from the video montage
along border strongholds
the rancor to delete
phone folders cameras
the burning compass
the palpable hallucination
a child struck deep
at the belly for the same
old rhetoric the same facts
useless to an emergency
are you in the hills, Ashur?
steely and bulletproof
the black oak shellskin
of the roadside corpse
not you not you but
freeze-framed to broker
the convivial oil deal
a pack full of joker cards
the mad dog's wheelmen
de-rig photo propagandas

he becalmed and resolute
jeeped in a spoof studio
not at the drum fields
pointing his rotten cane
who guards the pass there
only dust in the footages
leftover luggage
and the finger-wagging
send-in-the-marines
counter-bluff guzzled up
by SUV track distance
where I come back
blind after the dream
after the nightmare
to a dead phone line
to your epicurean face
missing in the crowd

# On the Cancellation of the Al-Sendian Festival

*for Rasha Omran*

Where a father laid out
    too soon tips the bird
        from the olive branch

And the cedar wood
    buckles under wind
        and laniaries of dust

Gut earth's bloodlock
    for toy silence in Tartous
        —the thresh of a sniper

On the mosque scaffold
    blurred and wracked
        by a prong of stars

Cold coins to the general
    low oud in the courtyard
        a widow's cello moan

And the bricked road
    and the red road banked
        by memorial flowers

And portraits of sons
    missing at the funeral
        undead at the checkpoint

At the rubbled amphitheatre
    where a soldier looks back
        from the black canvas

Juniper-eyed at the unmade
        window—a red eagle
                deadly to the throne

## Trinkets

*for Dragan Radovancevic*


Trinkets for your mother, a doctor
    in her own waiting room, juked
        by the dominion of a pancreas.

Trinkets over the bribe that punishes—
    a fair Dinar paid to brown the roses
        that bloom each day in her arteries.

Trinkets, anecdotes, anything but
    this betraying ivy that climbs
        through curtains of the hospice.

Trinkets to keep you going, friend
    at the worry stone, at the unknown
        country that is death, seen by her.

Trinkets scratched from the sun
    against your shade, not the oblique
        sympathy of the nurse at the tip tray.

Trinkets to light up the wickless room
    in Beograd and snuff the interminable
        reek of the zoo outside 'Pessoa Street.'

Trinkets for when the wind stops
    and a scent of omorika moves
        the green air over Fruska Gora.

## Bilu

Bilu—who gobbled up children for four thousand years
and stalked Dasagiri through the slopes of Mount Popa
booming the great gong of his voice—now folds / refolds
the blue-red silks of his democratic tie (demon-embossed)
and sends sudden felicitations to Venezuelan diplomats,
engineering execs from the Koreas and the febrile British.

Bilu fleecing the public bank account as he funnels off rice
in exchange for bottle factories (re-forged from the ghost
of abandoned Socialist factories). His children in the North
spray bullets at a blazing jungle, and in the South—uneaten,
but wholly devoured—they break rocks with their hands.

Bilu addresses the Western assembly in a tongue of whispers,
tells of how he has reformed from centuries of piling up bones,
while—in the East—a boy lights the matchbox of a minefield.

## The Old Men of Skopje Old Town

Landlocked, walled in where
the sea cannot settle them—
from lake clouds over Ohrid,
from the black eagle, *Shiptar*
whispered inside the shadow
of an arc lamp and the crude
standstill of a doorway. Men
plinthed on a beck of chairs
outside the bazaar, starching
black beards over checkers.
Or drowsy at the accordion,
thrown by day from the arms
of kohl-lined women who are
hollow from longing, heroines
like Calphurnia among Caesars,
amid the roar of heroic statues.

# The National Park

*for Sandeep*

Imperious eyes of the trained killer
draped in a white flag, who would
maculate us with the venom of his clan.

Here, where death is the stone inside
a rotting fruit; what would they ask
if not turning away at the final demand,

which is speech? They enter the gable
of the national park and do not tell us
and are with themselves and are gone.

## Night

*for Adonis*

Night, and the ripples of the river
float westwards, feebly arriving
on harbored ships at Lattakia;
the white sails rusted with blood.

Where exile is the prickly thorn
and the most rudimentary of flowers,
where a child scans the combusted
sky and knows himself in the night.

How to rinse out the ears of the world
so the world might see itself in this night?
How much of god in the mouth we kiss—
the dark mouth that is eating us alive?

## Fugitive

I trace the stacked
voices of shouters
how they immingle
with the vaporous
nick of taxis
gold-rushing the avenue
as if they were
part of the same
equation
(or miscalculation)
yet ruminantly fugitive
one or the other
sound falls back
to tundra distances
creating
double-choice
the street nerved
with intended pitch
and the aheadedness
of sound
being raked
into a kind of
sonic theatre
after leaving the ear
(or appearing
to leave)
where it encores
thread-frail
yet able enough
to jet the mind
for a second or more
undeserted
in the half-silence
as if nervously
retouched
to the shock of it

## Everything Broken Up Dances

1.

And what of the insatiable sadness of stepfathers

And her smeary mascara that slicks the rain

And the daub of red tape infecting a clean health bill

And what's with these singe-effects from the capitol bomb

And the dead telephone at the ear of a new generation

And when his welcoming smile widened like a crossbow

And how a wise oak lets in the new moon's eye

And the motel room with a stubbly kiss

And the jailbird in the yard firing rubber bullets

And the rotting fence surrounding the national comedy

And a white rosette for the bawdy little rich girl

And to wake after a decade shouting 'malady malady!'

And the weekday orgasm of the academic coming on a Sunday

And how the crucifiers were struck by womb lightning

And if the volcano would chirr just a little

And as they played jacks in the matron's office

And but for the sewage a smell of sweet sycamore

And the mind's polka played all through November

And the love gone to pot now cooks up the lobster

And with the years already shortening as it is

2.

When the heart sits down in its seat

When the temple wall sweated with blood

When you can take your gun and popcorn to the movie theatre

When the mind of the killer loaded buckle to belt

When the toddler scavenges in its own shit

When the riverbed is too dry to trickle downstream

When she said slavery was better off than these

When the tea party icebergs the senate

When the president waves a tar baby in the air

When kindness is the quilt that smothers you

When the desert sniper is perched above the border pass

When they load up a shopping basket and call it democracy

When at the crack of the starter pistol and the breaking of glass

When the prayer beads grind like teeth

When the sewer pipe spills with celebrity

When the hooray-henrys get chateau-faced

When entranced by the olympian flame sipping cold cola

When a life of exile is the new gap year

When the deal is tyrannicide per ton of crude oil

When the bodies went thump thump onto hard rock

3.

Or else god just loves a good thief

Or a buttery smile won't fill the pantry

Or because to breed them up is to breed us down

Or when there's nothing stranger than the rum of folk

Or when they die at noon they are born at midnight

Or what if the slum is only half frenzy

Or a fig-less Eve writhing your Eden

Or the schoolknife as the new son-of-a-gun

Or the library shelved with human ashes

Or the crazies in blue nightgowns at the ward gate

Or until this fable called history is agreed upon

Or to cut down the family forest is to preserve the tree

Or could it just be the bluster of jingoism

Or might Cicely and I inquire if you are fluent in African

Or when there's no change from the chameleons we voted in

Or in clean rags for a pail of water

Or as he cheated the wife's eye for the new cutie

Or as the prince was cracking eggs whilst listening to Handel

Or because it's different when the mutilated are Muslims

Or else what kind of sinner are you

4.

Yes the niblets surpass the dinner party anecdotes

Yes a little more bling might clinch the swing states

Yes the icicle-eyes of the ad-man are to warm you

Yes another day in the life of Adam and his pet snake

Yes the unopened page cannot be properly read

Yes a concrete staircase that can withstand a full-speed jet plane

Yes the hologram at the desk is your attentive web check-in

Yes the Ministry of Circuses is the Ministry of Culture

Yes Genghis Khan is buried here there and everywhere

Yes even the foulest water puts out the fiercest fire

Yes Hitler stroked his dog 'Wolf' in the bunker

Yes the art auctioneer is a punch-clock for the business tycoon

Yes a cargo-load of diplomacy to buy up the munitions site

Yes the church chandeliers can be seen as heavenly merchandise

Yes the librarian did it with the vicar in the green room

Yes just keep nodding along to the coffeepot bohemians

Yes we are living in the era of squeaky arses

Yes the tattoo above her buttocks reads DOGGY

Yes Artistic Impact woos the faculty committee

Yes nobody's perfect and he was just another nobody

5.

But for all the snowballs thrown in hell

But for every human grain in the Ganges

But the devil could give singing lessons to a voice like that

But the icecap reduced to a yellowy plume

But the louder they shout the less quietly we will come

But why do the dum-dums keep getting ahead

But they say dollars are better than real change

But what if the fifth commandment means Don't Trust Your Children

But brother fire says death is hereditary

But what if there was a law on hunger

But because the hardest thing in the world is to walk straight

But these summer rumba kids don't want to talk about it

But in Sanskrit the Empire ruled very differently

But why more admiral statues when the roads are so shoddy

But the electoral headwind is for fresh cuts

But the plucked eye on the end of a cocktail stick

But to know more intimately the murderer's brute joy

But the ewe licks the feet of the lion (its natural enemy)

But the gardener knows why the bud's heart is bloody

# Notes

"The Caprices":
These poems are a response to the Spanish artist Francisco y Lucientes Goya and his sequence titled *Los Caprichos*, first published in 1799 and consisting of eighty prints that depict various social caricatures, some involving monsters, asses, tricksters, and devils. The poem occasionally references commentaries that are alongside the original etchings, which were made by the artist and appear in his "Prado manuscript," housed in the Prado museum in Madrid.

"Isabella Stewart Gardner in Venice":
This title refers to an 1894 painting by Anders Zorn, which is of the same name as stated in the poem and hangs in the Isabella Gardner Museum in Boston, Massachusetts.

"Are you in the hills, Ashur?":
The poem refers to Colonel Gaddafi as "the mad dog," which is said to be the nickname that President Ronald Reagan devised for the former Libyan leader.

"On Hearing of the Cancellation of the Al-Sendian Festival":
The Al-Sendian Festival combined poetry, workshops, music, painting, and sculpture. Held annually for three days in the hills above Tartous in northern Syria, the festival was the idea of the late Mohamed Omran, who died after the opening year. His daughter Rasha kept Al-Sendian going for thirteen years until the violence in Syria brought about its closure, and Rasha was forced to live in exile.

"Trinkets":
The word "omorika" refers to "Picea omorika," common name of the Serbian spruce tree.

"Bilu":
A 'Bilu' is a mythological ogre or demon supposed to have roamed Burma in 2000 BCE.

"The Old Men of Skopje Old Town":
"Shqiptar" is an Albanian language ethnonym (autonym) that Albanians sometimes use to refer to themselves. A variant is "Shiptar," often used in a derogatory way by nationalist Serbians and Macedonians to refer to their Albanian neighbors.

## Acknowledgments

The author is grateful to the editors of the following journals and websites where some of these poems or earlier versions first appeared: archiveofthenow.org, *Axon, Blackbox Manifold, Black Herald, Cimarron Review, The Common, This Corner,* EYEWEAR, the blog (http://toddswift.blogspot.com), *Guernica, International Times, The Kenyon Review, Long Poem Magazine, Manhattan Review, Morning Star,* PEN America online (www.pen.org), Poetry International online (poetryinternational.org), *Prairie Schooner, Stand,* and *The White Review.*

"1977" and "Wild Desert Thyme" are included in *World English Poetry* (Bengal Publications, 2015), edited by Sudeep Sen.

"The Opponent" is included in *Dear World & Everyone In It* (Bloodaxe Books, 2013), edited by Nathan Hamilton.

"Bilu" and "Fragments for Ali" are included in *In Protest: 150 Poems for Human Rights* (Human Rights Consortium, University of London, 2013), edited by Helle Abelvik-Lawson, Anthony Hett, and Laila Sumpton.

"No Smoking" is included in *Lung Jazz: Young British Poets for Oxfam* (Cinnamon Press, 2012), edited by Todd Swift and Kim Lockwood.

"Cloud" is included in *Fragments of a Lost Voice: Poems for Harry Fainlight* (Iconoclast Press, 2011), edited by Dave Tomlin.

Thank you to New York University for a Stein Fellowship between 2010 and 2011. Also, thanks to the British Council for enabling the author to visit Syria (2009) and Burma (2013), and to Ashur Etwebi and Khaled Mattawa for arranging an invitation to the Tripoli International Poetry Festival in Libya (2012).

The author wishes to thank Ilya Kaminsky, Jim Schley, and Sandeep Parmar for their editorial suggestions when reading earlier versions of this collection.

## Other books from Tupelo Press

*See our complete list at www.tupelopress.org*